Toward a Theology of Santa Claus
a sermon by
Rev. Dorothy May Emerson

Copyright © Dorothy May Emerson
Sermon: "Toward a Theology of Santa Claus"
December 2017

All Rights Reserved
including the right of reproduction of this book,
copying, or storage in any form or means, including
electronic, without prior written permission of the author.

ISBN: 978-1-946088-06-2

1. Spirituality 2. Religion 3. Unitarian Universalism
4. Christmas 5. Feminist Theology 6. Title

Matrika Press
164 Lancey Street
Pittsfield, Maine 04967
(760) 889-5428
Editor@MatrikaPress.com

www.MatrikaPress.com

First Edition

Printed in the USA

a Sermon in My Pocket Series by Matrika Press

Matrika Press is delighted to present
this sermon by
Rev. Dorothy May Emerson
to be included in the
a Sermon in My Pocket Series

TOWARD A THEOLOGY OF SANTA CLAUS

Rev. Dr. Dorothy Emerson

It seems that everywhere you go these days Santa Claus is there.

Children swarm with delight around this comical figure, acting out a tradition that has become as much a part of the winter holiday season as Christmas carols, stories of the miraculous birth of the special baby Jesus, the lighting of the candles of Hanukkah and Kwanzaa, and the celebration of the Winter Solstice.

Most people think of the story of Santa Claus as something primarily for children, although anyone who has a young child knows how important this mythical figure can be, especially at this time of year.

You may wonder why I would choose to focus on this clearly secular story.

How could this possibly contribute to our spiritual understanding of the holiday season?

After all, aren't we supposed to delve into deeper issues in our worship?

Yet a common question asked about Santa Claus begins, "Do you believe in ... ?"

Because this question is also asked about God, we have the basis here for theological inquiry.

The word, theology means discourse, logos, on the divine, theos.

Anything that constitutes a matter of belief is a theological concern.

So, I invite us to explore dimensions of belief connected with Santa Claus, and to contemplate images of the divine to which this popular and pervasive figure might be related.

I must admit I've never really been a fan of Santa Claus.

I remember discovering the "truth" about Santa's identity at a very early age.

From then on I made sure that my younger brothers and sister and my own son were not duped into believing in this ridiculous figure.

Years later, I learned that despite the "truth" I had told my child, he decided to believe in Santa Claus, because all his friends did.

It's not that I mind Santa as a symbol.

In fact, in my family we sometimes sign our gift cards "Love, Santa."

My sister and I maintained a long tradition of "playing Santa" by filling Christmas stockings for each member of the family.

Because we were in Southern California and lived close to the church, we walked home from the Christmas Eve candle-light service at midnight with our candles still burning and tried to finish filling the stockings before the candles burned out.

Even in my adult life I still fill Christmas stockings for loved ones.

I must admit, too, that I love stories of Santa like Miracle on 34th Street, where the spirit of giving makes wondrous things possible, often in unexpected ways.

Such stories may focus on fulfilling the special wishes of children, wishes that can be quite unselfish in their expressions of love.

I appreciate this idea of Santa Claus as the spirit of giving and the special friend of children.

And yet, there is something that disturbs me about this legendary figure.

Years ago, when I was in Mexico, it occurred to me what the problem was.

In the iconography of many Mexican churches, there are pictures or statues on the two sides of the altar or of a rack of votive candles.

One side is dedicated to the Virgin Mary. On the other side are statues or pictures either of Jesus or of the Holy Trinity.

They didn't have pictures like that in the Presbyterian church of my youth. God and the Trinity were abstract concepts.

But looking at these Mexican Catholic images forced me to deal with the embodiment of the idea.

Then it struck me.

There was Santa Claus.

The father god was old white man with long white hair and a flowing white beard, just like Santa Claus, without the red suit of course.

Was this the god to whom I prayed as a child, asking for favors, begging for gifts, promising to be good?

Could he see me when I was sleeping?

Did he know when I was awake?

Did he really know if I'd been bad or good?

Just like Santa Claus?

This image of god, whether up in the sky or up at the North Pole, is clearly the god I don't believe in!

From a feminist perspective, we might critique this god/Santa Claus image for its gender exclusivity.

Because Santa takes the form of an old white man, there is an automatic exclusion of other manifestations of this spirit.

Sometimes there is a Mrs. Santa, but she is clearly a subsidiary figure, a helper to the big man, not a giver on her own.

One success of the move toward greater inclusivity has been to earn women and people of color the right, at least in some places, to don the red suit and play Santa for themselves.

But female Santas often still wear a long white beard, and Black Santas have flowing white hair, wavy perhaps, but never nappy. The costume, and the image, remains that of a white man.

Another disturbing factor in the portrayal of Santa Claus is the way this image is used to reinforce materialist values.

Some of you may be old enough to remember the TV sitcom Family Ties, or you may have seen the reruns.
The teenage boy Alex loves money and defends commercialism, so he yells "Stop!" anytime anyone even starts to talk about Santa Claus not being real.

To a child Santa Claus usually represents getting rather than giving.

Listen to children talking to their friends after Christmas Day.

The conversation often revolves around lists of what each child got in the way of presents.

Wouldn't it be nice, just once, to hear a list of what each child—or adult, for that matter—gave to others?

Perhaps most distressing of all, for anyone who finds the true meaning of Christmas in the story of the birth of the baby Jesus, is the way the figure and story of Santa Claus have eclipsed the focus on the Christ Child.

Ask most children who symbolizes the meaning of Christmas and my guess is you will find more who know Santa than who know Jesus.

One young friend of mine, when reminded about Christmas being the birthday of Jesus, remarked "Oh, yeah, that's the other story of Christmas."

Whether we like it or not, Santa is an inevitable part of this holiday season.

We can complain that the image and story of Santa Claus is inappropriate and even damaging, but there is no way we can get rid of it.

Like it or not, our children will see and hear stories, and they will meet this roly-poly man on the streets, in stores, at school and sometimes even at church.

So how, then, can we understand and use the story of Santa to support the values we hold dear?

Is there a Unitarian Universalist version of Santa Claus?

First, it is important to acknowledge the power of myth.

Over 100 years ago, in 1896, a columnist in Good Housekeeping magazine made the following wise suggestion:

> If the child is always told the myth of Santa Claus as a fairy tale, she will have all the childish joy and will have nothing to unlearn.
>
> You need not fear that he will lose the child's right to happiness in the story because of this way of presenting it.
>
> To a child of three, the spiritual is unintelligible, and the tale will be a simple actuality; when she reaches the age of five or six, her mind will readjust to an ideality.
>
> Tell the child the truth, by all means, but remember that for him, as for all

children, some of the deepest truths lie in the realm of fairy tale.

It is precisely because great truths are conveyed by myths and fairy tales that we must take the story of Santa Claus seriously.

One way to do this it to offer versions of Santa Claus in different forms, for instance, with different genders, skin colors, and body types.

Such reconstruction can affirm in an inclusive way the underlying spiritual message, the spirit of loving and giving, that Santa Claus can represent.

It may help to realize that our current image of Santa Claus originated, not in ancient mythology, but rather in the 19th century.

The primary sources of our contemporary image of Santa appear to be

Clement Moore's poem, "A Visit from St. Nicholas," first published in 1823, and the drawings of cartoonist Thomas Nast, which appeared in Harper's Weekly every year from 1863 to 1902.

By the beginning of the 20th century the American image and story of Santa Claus had been fixed in the popular mind and have varied little since then.

Realizing that this image was created at a specific time empowers us to recreate the story in a form of our own choosing, in a way that reflects our current values.

Tracing the lineage of Santa Claus' predecessors in earlier times and across many lands takes us on a fascinating cross-cultural journey.

The story of a kind and generous being who comes at the coldest time of the year to bring joy and love to children and to those in need is apparently more universal than it might at first seem.

It is as if the human psyche needs to personify a vision of warmth and comfort to help people survive the cold of winter.

Not surprisingly, the most powerful and pervasive stories come from the coldest most northern regions of Europe, although there are related stories from the south as well.

Feminist theology also teaches us to suspect that behind every patriarchal male god image there is probably an earlier female one.

Santa is no exception.

One way to discover the deeper meaning of the symbol of Santa Claus may be to go back and learn some of the earlier stories.

The first Santa Claus may have been the goddess Hertha or Ertha, also known as Mother Earth.

This northern Germanic goddess visited people all over the world, riding in her sacred car, drawn by a team of heifers.

Wherever she went, she brought rejoicing and festivity.

While she visited, all weapons of war were locked away. Fighting stopped while warring tribes joined together to worship the goddess.

Then there's the Russian story of Babushka, the Grandmother, who was invited to travel with the three wise men, when they stopped at her house on their way to find the Christ Child.

But Babushka was afraid of strangers and didn't like the idea of traveling on a cold night.

Later she regretted her decision not to go along and set out to look for the child on her own.

She is said to wander through Russia all winter long, but on Christmas Eve, with her old apron filled with candy and toys, people invite her into their homes to delight the children.

Befana's story also relates to the Magi. The Italian legend tells of the wise men visiting her on their way to find Jesus.

She wanted to go with them, but she had to finish her work first. When she got done with her sweeping, she tried to catch up with them, but she couldn't find them or the child.

So now she rides through the air on her broomstick, searching for the Christ Child in every home she passes.

She goes down each chimney and leaves gifts for the children by the manger scenes they have set up.

Befana is often pictured as a fairy queen, or perhaps a good witch.

The gifts of the Magi to Jesus serve as one precedent for the giving of gifts to children at Christmas.

It is interesting that the three kings give their gifts to one who is also called by royal titles—King of the Jews, Prince of Peace.

The women, on the other hand, who might be said to represent various female aspects of the divine, bring their gifts to all children, as do their descendants in the form of Santa Claus.

The other exception is the Spanish story of Balthazar, one of the Magi, who brings gifts to many children.

He places the gifts in shoes or boots that are left out on Christmas Eve, often near chimneys.

Balthazar also provides us with a model for a Black Santa, as he is often pictured with dark skin.

In Germany, Kris Kringle was originally female, possibly an angel.

There are still some German families in which one of the women dresses in white with golden wings.

She climbs in the window and waits by the Christmas tree for the children to come in and receive their gifts.

The name Kris Kringle probably came from the term Christ Child—Christ Kindlein, in German.

Indeed, early images of Santa Claus in Germany were often accompanied by the image of the baby Jesus.

The symbolic nature of the Christ as the ultimate gift of God to humankind is another aspect of the love and giving now represented by Santa Claus.

Then there's the 4th century saint who is called Nicholas, and who is therefore assumed to be the forerunner of Santa Claus.

The fact that many shrines to Saint Nicholas were formerly temples of Poseidon suggests his origin as the god of the sea who had earlier replaced Artemis as protector of sailors.

Saint Nicholas was also known as protector of the weak against the strong, the poor against the rich, the servant and slave against the master.

In this role, his alliance with the oppressed parallels that of Jesus.

Also like Jesus, who invited the children to come to him, Nicholas is known as the patron saint of children.

My favorite story of Santa Claus was published in 1932. It's called The Life and Adventures of Santa Claus, written by Julie Lane. The introduction reads:

> Draw close to the fire, all you who believe in the spirit of Christmas, whether you call it Santa Claus, or simply good will to [ail]; and listen to the story of Nicholas the Wandering Orphan who became Nicholas the Wood-Carver, a lover of children. Follow him through his first years as a lonely little boy, who had the knack of carving playthings for children; then as a young man, busy over the little toys; then as a prosperous, fat, rosy old man, who overcomes all sorts of difficulties in order to attain his ambition, a toy for every child in the village.

In this charming and touching story Santa Claus becomes a real person, one who dedicates his life to sharing his gifts with others. It makes Santa into a role model we would all do well to emulate.

When we gather all these stories together, we find that Santa Claus is much more complex and more significant religiously than contemporary characterizations would suggest.

Perhaps the stories of Jesus and Santa Claus are not so incompatible after all.

When we consider the deeper meanings and the wider sources of this beloved Christmas figure, we discover the spirit of loving and giving in many forms.

There is no need to limit Santa Claus to a roly-poly old white man in a red suit.

Santa can be anyone.

The essential element is the importance of giving, especially to children.

Surely this concurs with our values as Unitarian Universalists.

As we celebrate this joyous season, let us open our hearts and our lives to the joy of giving.

We can take on the image of Santa Claus for ourselves.

Each of us can become the spirit of love. In so doing, we make real the divine within.

As Carter Heyward puts it:
> God is nothing other than the eternally creative source of our relational power, our common strength, a god whose movement is to empower, bringing us into our own together, a god whose name in history is love.

The holidays give us a chance to practice being who we could be for the rest of our lives.

Rev. Dorothy May Emerson is an ordained Unitarian Universalist minister who leads seminars for Rainbow Solutions, a socially responsible investing firm in Medford, Massachusetts.

She is the author and editor of many books including, Crone Curriculum: Becoming Women of Wisdom; Glorious Women: Award-Winning Sermons about Women; A Matter of Preference: A Book About the Myers-Briggs Type Indicator; and several volumes of UU history, including Standing Before Us: Unitarian Universalist Women and Social Reform, 1776-1936 (Skinner House, 1999).

Matrika Press is pleased to be publishing her soon to be released memoir entitled:

SEA CHANGE 1960s: The Unfinished Agenda, an intimate exploration of a young life lived on the edge of radical hope, change, and possibility in the 1960s in California.

www.MatrikaPress.com/dorothy-may-emerson

Matrika Press is an independent publishing house dedicated to publishing works in alignment with Unitarian Universalist values and principles.
Its fiscal sponsor is UU Women and Religion.
(www.uuwr.org)

Matrika derives its name from the 50 letters of the Sanskrit alphabet called "the mothers" aka "Matrika." Kali Ma used the letters to form words, and from the words formed all things... as with the Bible: *"in the beginning was the Word."*
People of all backgrounds and faiths agree: *Words are powerful.*
More than that: *Their vibrations are creative forces; they bring all things into being.*

Matrika Press publishes anthologies, memoirs, poetry, prayer and ritual manuscripts, and other books to bring transformation to the world.

We *do* accept unsolicited manuscripts at this time.
Should you wish to publish your work, please visit our website.

www.MatrikaPress.com

FIND OUT HOW
YOUR CONGREGATION OR GROUP *CAN HOST*
a local UU Talks in your community. UU Talks is a
speakers series, similar to TED Talks, where Speakers
will speak about topics aligned with UU Values.
Join Us!
www.UUTalks.org

*Above pictured: Inaugural UU Talks event
at the UUA Boston, 2017*
*Peter Bowden, Matt Meyer, Lydia Edwards, Rev. Allison Palm,
Jim Tull, Anna Huckabee Tull, Regie Gibson, Marlon Carey,
Rev. Hank Pierce, "Twinkle" Marie Manning*

AVAILABLE NOW FROM MATRIKA PRESS

This book is a compilation of women sojourners, sages, mystics, witches, shaman, medicine women, ministers, philosophers, therapists, life coaches, yogis, and more. Their journeys. Their stories. Their teachings and practices. Essays, Poetry, Art, Rituals and Prayers. This anthology is full of useful tools and powerful messages for everyone who is on a spiritual journey to embrace and enjoy. Beloved Contributors include:
- *Anna Huckabee Tull • Bernadette Rombough • Deb Elbaum*
- *Deborah Diamond • Debra Wilson Guttas • Grace Ventura*
- *Janeen Barnett • JoAnne Bassett • Judy Ann Foster*
- *Julie Matheson • Kate Early • Kate Kavanagh • Katherine Glass*
- *Kris Oster • Lea M. Hill • Meghan Gilroy • Morwen Two Feathers*
- *Rustie MacDonald • Shamanaca • Sharon Hinckley • Shawna Allard*
- *Shiloh Sophia • Susan Feathers • Tiffany Cano • Tory Londergan*
- *"Twinkle" Marie Manning • Tziporah Kingsbury • Valerie Sorrentino*

www.MatrikaPress.com